CROWN OF THORNS

ANTHOLOGY OF WAR POEMS

DARSHIT PANDIT

For the veterans of war, the spreaders of peace, and those who forever carry the flames of hope in their heart.

Contents

1. When he came from war

World War 1

His face looks like a veteran's
He should be proud
But why does he look
As though he weaved a shroud?
His face looks gaunt
And his eyes look red
Does he find his eyelids stained
With all the blood he shed?
Something inside him changed
Or rather something broke?
We all are around him
But did he befriend smoke?
He's no longer the man
We knew when he left
When he came back home
Is of care he bereft?
What has happened to him?
I want to find the one I knew
But a shroud of his past
Should I start to sew?

2. Falling Embers

Falling embers
Horrors of skies
When we look at the world
We all tell lies
Like a cloaked figure in gold
But hands reek of death
It will devour all
Futile is your sheath
Like a fiery ball of gold
It swoops from the skies
Against your life
The ember vies
There is no escape
There is no choice
Crushed into silence
Will be your voice
Crushed like a flame
Consumed by a fire
As life slips away
Flames go higher and higher
Burnt without mercy
Encased in flames
War memorials look serene

But ashes bear no names
Turned to dust
Ash and smoke
The ground of war
In blood they soak
They turn into embers
Of fury and pain
Wishes, blessings, prayers
They all go in vain
They cry out in agony
But they die in glory
Immortal is their names
Immortal their story

3. When the Duke went for a ride

World War 1

It was a fateful day
When the Duke went for a ride
The moment everything changes
When he and his family died
Germany and Austria Hungary
Together were on war's door
Relied on Russia being late
Which resulted in gore
Britain was a friend of France
Russia And Serbia allied
Whereas Belgium was tentative
But took France's side
Germany won an early victory
Tannenberg, they won
And soon Belgium was
Going to be in front of guns
Trying to invade France
But the fortresses were too strong
And then Germany struck
On Belgium, the war gong
Belgians were brutally killed

Innocent blood was shed
To save them and France
Britain was going to head
On the edge of River Marne
The invasion was halted
Since it was the east of Paris
Germany's wound was salted
Germany and Austria-Hungary
Got attacks from east and west
They had to build the trench
They had stopped seeing rest
Britain, Australia and New Zealand
Attacked Ottoman, which had had time to bide
It resulted in casualties
Many of their men died
Germany attacked at Verdun
The defence he wanted to break
The army fought brutally
For so much was at stake
They were forced to retreat
The armies had no choice
Their own screams were subduing
In the French's voice
The 'Big Push' began
It tried to break the Somme lines
Many troops were shot
Of defeat, it showed signs

After attacks on American ships
Finally, USA entered the war
They planned 'Hundred Days Offensive'
That was what they were there for
Finally, the foe surrendered
And thus ended the first world war
If the Austrian had known
What it had all been for
Maybe there wouldn't
Have been such a big war

4. And Hiroshima never saw sleep

Hiroshima nuclear attack

One day all the world
Forever any sleep
I was a fire wild
A tsunami deep
Till the darkest hour
All Japan was quiet
No sign of a struggle
No sign of a fight
There was a sudden light
Like the sun had stepped down
It was blinding
Dazzled the whole town
And then everything blew apart
Buildings started to collapse
As the fiery ball was swelling
And their memory went through a lapse
When the citizens woke up
There was fire all around
Everything was engulfed in fire
Corpses were abound
People were slain to radiation

Or were lost to fire
Or they were the one to earn
The Gamma Ray's ire

5. With their scarlet hands

Hiroshima Bombing

A song of death
Or a song of sorrow
A world of strife
A cloud without skies
How could they sleep?
How did they cry?
No tears could come
There was only dust
No dad or ma
Gone in Hiroshima
How could they sleep
With their scarlet hands
The birth of death
And the death of born
When the cries loud
Etched themselves
What did dream
A cruel feat?
Innocent sake
Blood in lakes
If they just made peace
If they could live

But with guilty souls
They shall know
How guilt is death
How death is the end
How the end is dust
And the blood they shed in the dust
The innocent blood
Stained their hands
Nothing could reverse it
Just sleepless nights and penance
Someday, they would regret
Feel remorse and realize
How guilt is death
Over and over again

6. A Volley of embers

Yogendra Singh Yadav- The Kargil War

Holding death in those hands
I climb to the summit
One wrong step
And to my death I would plummet
From my hands I launch
I send a lethal ghoul
An ember ready to swoop
On the enemy's soul
But the foe mustn't see me
Or I shall meet my end
They can kill me if they must
But I shall never bend
As I climb upon the hill
My life knows no fear
I am only to defend
The country I hold dear
Preparing for the attack
The enemy shan't be back
The steep paths we climb on
Are ready for us to slip
Roots snake across the hill
Inviting us to trip

A tiny tent we see
The refuge of the foe
As we approach in their vicinity
Our footsteps go slow
With the embers of death
And the silence of hell
A place belonging to us
Where our countrymen fell
As I think of the enemy
Infinite fury fills my blood
Many people they killed
Massacred like a flood
The fire's about to touch the ground
Better unleash the wild hellhound
And as the wrath of the embers
Visits upon the tent
A volley of bombs
Our way is sent
Embers of fire
And clouds of screams
Their plan to capture us
Shall always remain a dream
A rain of bullets
Thunders upon my men
As the foe runs
And hides in the den
A bullet comes my way

And I know how this must end
They can kill me if they must
But I shall not bend
But before I bit adieu
A task needs to be done
I threw a grenade on their bunks
And now, they run
But as I fall on the ground
Is it really death?
Hands are on my forehead
Feeling like a wreath
And I still breathe
But everyone thinks I'm no more
Perhaps now is the time
To write a new page in the lore

7. Fate's Amend

My hands are shivering
When I look at the sea
Something tells me to run
Something tells me to flee
Something is severely wrong
A danger I sense
Something is approaching
Near that fence
Where the sea ends
From where the ships sail
There is a grey airship
Blows a swift gale
I rush to the headquarters
For I see more
There are six in the skies
Like death at the door
They were great fiery spheres
Like the gongs of end
Plummeting like burning steeds
Fate had finally brought an amend

8. Gone Forever

Nagorno-Karabakh Conflict

A little house is all we have
With crumbling walls
We never know
When it falls
There was a garden
And we had a life
Till the war came
And tore us like a knife
The Drones will come any moment
And end our days
And we'd never see
The sun-kissed rays
A little missile would come
With a cluster of bombs
They would kill us all
Without ashes for tombs
They would fire from the mulch
And everything would be gone
Every man and woman
Would be burnt to the bone
A trivial fight
For a piece of land

Our lives would be snatched
By their hands
The missile in the air
A cluster of bombs fall
And that is the moment
When dark swallows all

9. Fire the Canons

"Russian-Ukraine War"

His face left life
His eyes parted with the light
Day happens above me
But in my heart, it's all night
Those we knew
Are all gone
Their hearts turn to smoke
I'm a soldier lone
Fire the Cannons
For mortal are lives
No one knows
Who survives
We turn to blood
We have to, we must
For the word of a royal man
We all turn to dust
His breath goes still
His heart ceases to beat
We don't know where to go
We forgot how to eat

But who cares? Lives are mortal
The Cannons must be fired
For all the lives we tore
All the blood we acquired
Men die all the time
Governments fall
Mortal are lives
We must answer the call
People die hungry
Or die inspired
All they know
The Cannons must be Fired

10. Crown of Thorns

After the war ended
The field yielded blood
Ashes and smoke
Was reaped from the mud
All the deaths
The gore and cries
For the Crown of Gold
A glory made of lies
The stones of the castle
Were made of ashes
A throne taken away
After countless clashes
But the truth, is that
The crown, your head which adorns
Is the dream of bloodshed
A Crown of Thorns
A Crown that
Sits upon your head
It engraves the cries
Of the innocent who bled
The curses on you
Of the blood soaked in your soil
It's not a medal

Nor is it a war's spoil
After all the blood was shed
Of theirs and yours
What you have got?
Do the glories obscure?
You have got a kingdom
That is made of pain
A reign of terror
Where humanity was slain
But the truth, is that
The crown, your head which adorns
Is the dream of bloodshed
A Crown of Thorns

The Beginning Of A New Anthology

An excerpt from the upcoming book...

And when they came back
The merry dream broke
All that was left
Was sorrow and smoke
It was a night of new moon
Heralding a bright light
But until it came
It was a dark night

9 798886 678567

Printed by Libri Plureos GmbH in Hamburg,
Germany